IMAGES
of America

AROUND
CENTRAL ISLIP

Sr. Anne Frances Pulling, RSM

The building of many lives, lives on. This was Lowton's private home on southwest Suffolk Avenue before the building was moved to Carlton Avenue in 1919. It became Koch's home and general store, Bernsteins Dry Goods store in 1923, and Carlton's 5 & 10 in 1940. The Central Islip Public Library was housed here from 1953 until 1976. The building was then revitalized by the Thermalume Construction Co. and transformed into offices. It continues in that capacity.

COVER: The first train running under the East River tunnel.

IMAGES
of America

AROUND
CENTRAL ISLIP

Sr. Anne Frances Pulling

ARCADIA

First published 1998
Copyright © Sr. Anne Frances Pulling, 1998

ISBN 0-7524-0492-X

Published by Arcadia Publishing,
an imprint of the Chalford Publishing Corporation,
One Washington Center, Dover, New Hampshire 03820.
Printed in Great Britain

Library of Congress Cataloging-in-Publication Data applied for

Dedicated to my parents, Josiah and Mary Mernin Pulling;
my sister and brother, Almira and Ezra;
my grandfather, Dr. Ezra R. Pulling, who introduced our family to Central Islip;
and my grandmother, Delia Broderick Pulling,
who instilled in me a love of local history and the desire to preserve it.

Almira Pulling, Bernard Simms, and Mary Boyle are intrigued by a new horseless carriage during a visit to Coney Island. This new innovative mode of transportation entered the village scene when McBreen's Hudson chugged along Carlton Avenue's clamshell road in 1916.

Contents

Acknowledgments

This publication is based on research, records, documents, newspapers, and interviews with townsfolk, many of whom generously supplied information and offered constructive suggestions. A special thank you goes to Anne Pavlak and Paul Facchiano of the Central Islip Public Library for their assistance and to Murial Remsen of the former State Hospital Archives, for sharing many photographs along with her wealth of knowledge. Thanks to photographer Phyllis M. Mantuori of the New York Institute of Technology for sharing campus photographs.

A word of gratitude goes to Nancy Manfredonia and the Central Islip Civic Council, Dr. Andrew Schwartz and the Central Islip Chamber of Commerce, Fr. Bruce Reed, Michael and Audrey Krumenaker, Ruth McCalla, and Islandia Town Hall. I wish to acknowledge the collections of Ron Ziel, The Smithtown Historical Society, and Noel J. Gish. I am grateful to The Long Island Catholic, Sr. Marie Halligan R.C., and Sr. Patricia Manning, C.S.J. A word of appreciation goes to Principal John Cassidy, Mary Herrera, John and Neil Finnan, and Joan Oscar.

A prayerful gratitude goes to all who assisted in any way by supplying photographs, constructive suggestions, proofreading, etc. It is because of your gracious preservation of Central Islip history that we bridge the gap between past and future. I am especially grateful to my own religious community, The Sisters of Mercy of the Dallas Regional Community, for their support and encouragement in this project.

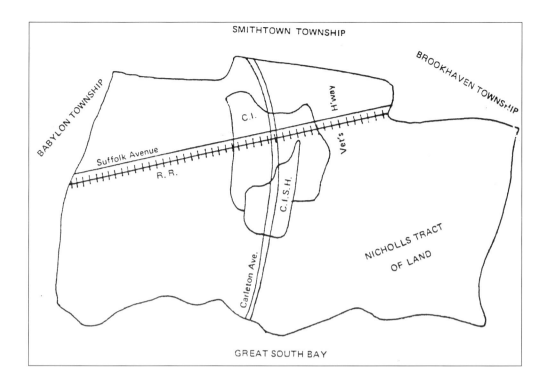

SMITHTOWN TOWNSHIP

Introduction

Our little hamlet on the Long Island plains, where the scrub oak and pine barren belts overlap, was part of the Nicholl Patent. In 1683 William Nicholl bought an 8-by-10-mile tract of land from Winnequaheagh, Grand Sachem of the Connequot Indians. His famous estate was called "Islip" after his ancestral home in England. Long Island was originally inhabited by 13 peaceable tribes of Native Americans. The first and main line of the Long Island railroad had just reached eastward into Nicholl's tract of land by 1842 and Suffolk Station was established at the present Islip Avenue crossing. This site had became a central core for neighboring settlements where stage and rail met; hence the area centralized around the station became Central Islip. Thirty years later the station was transferred a mile east when land was deeded for that purpose.

In 1848 George K. Hubbs of Smithtown bought 939 acres of land and built his home on a picturesque, rustic road called Suffolk Avenue. He regarded the crossroads east of his home as a future hub of activity since its lanes led in all directions. Tramped out in earlier times by Native Americans, the North Lane became Wheeler Road, named for his wife, Ruth Wheeler. Hubbs and his family of five were the hamlet's first settlers. His original house is presently preserved on Dow Street. Two years later their first neighbors were welcomed. The William Stokes family of Nottingham, England, settled east of Hubbs. English settlers and pioneers of English descent came in rapid succession to make their homes in the dense woodlands. The pine air was deemed healthful and the soil fertile for agriculture. The earliest names crossing the pages of our history were Holmes, Adams, Saddington, Lowton, and Powell. The pioneers had laid the foundation of a thriving settlement, and the little village of 150 inhabitants was quite content as the 20th century approached. A major turn of events yet undreamed of in the little hamlet would soon take place.

In 1887 the railway to the east brought another group of incoming dwellers. City hospitals for the mentally incompetent were becoming overcrowded and manual work was recognized as therapy. The little village, just over one hour from New York City, was deemed "The Promised Land" when the Commissioner of Charity and Correction bought 1,000 acres south of the railroad and established New York State Farm Colony. Plans were drawn up for three groups of one-story buildings called A, B, and C. On May 6, 1889, the first residents, 140 men, arrived. They cleared the land and planted grain. Menial household tasks needed attention so the following summer women were included. Dr. George McDonald was the first director. In 1905 the farm colony became independent and was renamed Central Islip State Hospital. Resident population increased which necessitated additional help. Townsfolk were settled in their own pursuits. An invitation echoed across the sea to the newspapers of Ireland. "Come to Central Islip, Good Work, Good Pay"! The response was irresistible. Thirty, of thirty-two counties in Ireland, would be represented in the village and among the employees of the local establishment over the next three decades. In 1955 there were ten thousand patients with two thousand employees. Irish immigration declined following the Depression and children of our earliest immigrants gradually filled the positions of their parents. Following World War II the village underwent a cultural evolution. The Irish have valiantly left us a rich heritage of courage, fortitude, and perseverance.

The abandoned source of income resulting from decentralization of the hospital in 1955 created a degenerative effect in the village. Michael A. LoGrande, planning director and Islip town supervisor, searched for a prestigious university that would serve as an anchor for new research and development. In 1983 the New York Institute of Technology, which was founded in Westbury in 1955, bought most of the buildings and land vacated by the hospital. The following year the Central Islip Campus opened with 350 students. The goal of the New York Institute of Technology is to offer a modern campus for five thousand students with programs in partnership with the business sector. The college has been the economic catalyst for the community sparking rehabilitation in all areas of the village. Tech Park demonstrates the unique transformation of an archaic institution into a world model of public and private partnership! It exhibits the adaptive reuse of the hospital into a planned, diversified community of the 20th century. The rapid succession of amenities surrounding this venture is astounding.

Ambitious plans gained momentum when Carlton Park, once a blighted neighborhood, was transformed into an area of beautiful, affordable homes and winding lanes. Known as College Woods, it attracts young, low and middle-income families as well as those who seek employment in any of the many new industries that surround the college. Park Row is an attractive series of town houses designed in accord with campus architecture. They utilize the natural beauty of the land. Many stately old trees have been preserved and enhance the charm of the development. The ethnic background of Central Islip is so diverse that cultural backgrounds can be traced to nearly every country of the world. Diversity makes the village unique! Mixed income, background, and race blend into one small hamlet of 27,000 of which one third each are black, Hispanic, and white. "Diversity is a strength of Central Islip."

Revitalization was not limited to any one area. Electrification of the railroad in 1988 with less than an hour service to Manhattan and the widening of Carlton and Suffolk Avenues gave the area a needed thrust. The Cohalan Court Complex and the Federal Courts gave it an impetus long overdue. Central Islip is a modern renaissance village that seems to grow younger the older it gets.

One

A Glimpse of Yesteryear

The Central Islip railroad station was originally located at Islip Avenue. In 1842 the railroad was extended eastward to that site. In 1873 George K. Hubbs, the first resident in the hamlet, deeded land for the railroad station across from his home. Located on the southwest corner of Wheeler Road and Suffolk Avenue it became a hub of activity and served the village for nearly eight decades.

George K. Hubbs was our first white settler. He, with his family of five, came from Smithtown in 1848 and built a home on west Suffolk Avenue. Hubbs was a school inspector, teacher, constable, and justice of the peace. He established the first general store, which was located on the southwest corner of Suffolk Avenue and Wheeler Road. In 1873 he deeded land for a railroad station.

This is the oldest house in the village! Built by George K. Hubbs in 1848 on Suffolk Avenue, facing the railroad, it stood approximately where McDonalds restaurant is today. In 1957 the historic landmark was moved across Zorn's Poultry Farm to Dow Street where it is preserved as a residence. The first telephone exchange was located in this building.

This is the original establishment of Henry Holmes. A merchant from Grantham, England, Holmes settled on the northeast corner of Wheeler Road and Suffolk Avenue in 1858. He built a home and operated a general store and coal business. In 1902 his establishment was struck by lightning and demolished. Holmes, our second English newcomer, was preceded only by Thomas Stokes, who settled here in 1850.

This building was a familiar site for many years. Holmes rebuilt his establishment on the same site and resumed business. His home became a landmark, later serving as the Dr. Earl McCoy residence. It was demolished to make way for a mini mall built by Harold McGowan in 1946. Following World War I, a park was dedicated on the opposite corner; townsfolk are shown here gathering for the festivities.

The Episcopal church was the first house of worship in the village. Henry Homes donated property on Church Street and the edifice was erected there in 1869. It served for a half century. Then the hub of activity shifted. In 1923 the wooden frame church was moved, and still functions 12 decades later. The Guild Hall, originally built by the church on Suffolk Avenue, underwent many evolutions over the next six decades.

The Episcopal church shown in its new setting in 1923. It was moved to the southwest corner of Brightside and Carlton Avenues. An oblong building was brought from Nicoll Road to serve as a parish hall. The church was covered with stucco and a fence enclosed the complex. The site was originally owned by the Gissell family.

The Methodist church was established in 1870. George K. Hubbs donated one plot for a cemetery and church when William Sheppard came to the village fired with zeal for the spread of Methodism. The church was erected at a cost of $1,500 of which Sheppard contributed $900. By 1910 the membership reached ten families. Mary Bridger was the organist for both the Episcopal and Methodist congregations.

Thomas Bridger was the first pioneer to develop land south of the railroad. In 1857 he came from Ossining, New York, in quest of pinelands. He constructed a residence on Brightside Avenue which is still in use. Education began in a room over Bridger's Carpenter Shop in 1857 with Catherine Homan as the teacher of 15 pupils.

The little schoolhouse of 1861 was built on Wheeler Road. In 1860 George K. Hubbs donated an acre of land to Union Free School District #13 at the present Alfano School site. Smith R. Rippingale was awarded the contract to construct a brick school. Later, he settled on Wheeler Road.

In 1904 a two-room schoolhouse was erected to accommodate the rising population. William Russell, an early janitor, was hired to clear ashes, light the stove, clear the woodshed, and prune trees. In those days a bench and desk went for $25, a dustpan and broom for 50¢, and a stovepipe cost $1.50. The stove itself cost $7.

14

The students of Central Islip School gathered for a photograph in 1904. From left to right they are as follows: (front row) unidentified, George Staups, Ruth Hatch, Mary A. Miller, Grace Hubbs, Albert Miller, Pheobe Homes, and Henry Hines; (top row) teacher Bernice Monk, Mrs. William Davis, and the Marshall brothers.

The two-story, four-classroom school of 1913 has survived many generations of students. Three schools have stood on the same acre of land donated by George K. Hubbs—the little schoolhouse of 1866, the wooden frame building of 1890, and the two-story brick edifice of 1913. This building will endure for it is now part of Alfano School.

Suffolk Avc., Central Islip, L. I.

This is Suffolk Avenue as seen from the corner of Wheeler Road. Notice the fence around the Episcopal church on the left and the roof of Guild Hall are both partially hidden by Nelson's Bike Shop. The hall was originally part of the Episcopal parish.

This is the first medical office in the hamlet. In 1892 Dr. Ezra R. Pulling rented a house on Oakdale Avenue and set up medical practice. He traveled twice weekly from New York City to serve the townsfolk. He later purchased the premises, built a little house just east of his office, and moved his family to the then quiet, little village.

Dr. Ezra R. Pulling was the first physician for the settlers. A NYC surgeon, he came at the invitation of a colleague. He had been a medical officer in the General Hospital at Newark, a surgeon at Ft. Watsworth, had taught medicine and pathology at the University of New York, and received an honorary degree from the Medical Society of New York.

Delia Broderick Pulling was our first Irish settler. Born in Galway, Ireland, she was a seamstress and clothing designer for Gimbel's Department Store on Fifth Avenue. She became the wife of Dr. Ezra Pulling and moved to Central Islip in 1893. This photograph, with her youngest son, Josiah, was taken in 1902. She was the first of over 300 Irish immigrants who would relocate from the Emerald Isle to Central Islip.

17

The first train to emerge from the East River Tunnel arrived on September 8, 1910. It was greeted with much applause at each Long Island railroad station along the main line, as it heralded a direct link with Pennsylvania Station and New York City! Access through the East River Tunnel meant faster and more efficient travel. It meant "Change at Jamaica" or switching engines, but the convenience to passengers was tremendous.

Horse sheds were located behind the railroad station. Originally built in 1879, as a protection for horses owned by railroad passengers, it became a garage when Dobbin was replaced by cars!

A Winter Sce...

Hilliards Farm
Wheeler Rd. approx 1908

George Hilliard bought the house and barn of Hezekiah Hatch in the 1860s. Located east of the Methodist church, the house and farm faced Wheeler Road on the corner of Hilliard Street. Hezekiah, who owned sugar plantations in Cuba, was the father of Samuel Hatch, caretaker of the Slater estate.

This carriage is traveling north on Wheeler Road in 1915. The yet unpaved thoroughfare was named by Hubbs for his wife, Ruth Wheeler. Our earliest pioneers lived north of the railroad. Hilliard, a New York financier, settled the road named for him.

The mail wagon from the local hospital waits by the general store for the train. Built by Hubbs in the late 1800s, the building also served as the first post office in the village. It was located on the southwest corner of Wheeler Road and Suffolk Avenue and eventually evolved into Johnson's garage.

Many fine businesses populated Carlton Avenue in 1915. The Ken Long Pharmacy, Ryan's Candy Kitchen, and the Robert Donohue Building were all demolished in the great fire of 1918. Donohue rebuilt and Ryan relocated across the street. Carlton Avenue was a clamshell road until 1921.

The fire department was established in 1905 with a horse-drawn ladder and pump. Unfortunately, the department did not own a horse, so the first man to arrive with a team of horses, after the alarm sounded, received a bonus of $5. The alarm was the church bell. The original firehouse housed two firetrucks. The building was demolished for the widening of Suffolk Avenue.

The St. John of God Church became a reality in 1903. A frame Romanesque edifice was constructed midway between the railroad station and the hospital grounds. In 1904 St. John of God officially became a parish. Rev. Nicholas Keating was its first resident pastor.

This was a typical Sunday scene in 1906. Looking south from Wheeler Road visitors arrive on the Long Island railroad and hike the mile south to the state hospital. Fisher's Hotel is in the background. In inclement weather a horse and buggy transported the visitors and eventually taxi service became available. In those days there were between 200 and 300 visitors each Sunday.

Fisher's Hotel was built by John T. Fisher in 1886. Originally a white building, it was located just south of the railroad station and served as a landmark for over eight decades. It will be fondly remembered as the bus stop of an earlier era. It was razed to make way for a park.

The blacksmith shop was originally owned by Robert Holmes. He operated it near his Uncle Henry's home, at the crossroads, until 1905, when Henry Hines bought the smithy. In 1928 Hines moved it behind his home where it remained in operation until mid-century. The horseless carriage had taken over by then and horses were no longer performing the work of their ancestors. The blacksmith shop is currently back in operation.

This is the home of Samuel Hatch. Once situated on the northeast corner of Wheeler Road and Suffolk Avenue, it is preserved on Dow Street. In 1875 James Slater established a 150-acre estate on the east side of Carlton Avenue. His wife, Alice, named the street in front of their mansion Brightside Avenue. When the estate was destroyed by fire, Fisher laid out the acreage into First, Second, and Third Avenues. This was Central Islip's closest touch of the Gold Coast.

John and Helen Smith settled on Adams Road in 1857. A half century later, on June 2, 1907, their golden wedding anniversary was celebrated. They had six girls: Alice, Marie, Annie, Jennie, Kitty, and Nora. Those present were, from left to right, as follows: (front row) Steve Dougherty, Katherine Smith McGuire, Annie Smith Dougherty, Mildred McGuire, Marguerite Edwards, and James Haggerty; (second row) Marie Smith, Helen Smith, John Smith, Jennie, and Fred McGuire; (third) Henry Edwards, Annie Adams Dougherty, Mrs. Alfred Adams, Kitty Smith, Mrs. Van Nostrand, Nora Edwards, Grace Dougherty, Josephine Just, and Jennie Smith; (back row) Herbert Dougherty, Alfred Adams, Mrs. Edwards, Mr. Edwards, Fred McGuire, Father Keating, Frank Edwards, and Mary Haggerty. This is the first recorded golden wedding anniversary in the village.

Dobbin the horse trots north at the crossroads of Carlton and Suffolk Avenues. Veteran's Park, housing the monument to the servicemen of World War I, stands on the southeast corner. The Crozier Building and the original firehouse are in the background.

A barn dance took place in Hoyt's barn on Suffolk Avenue in 1915. This was the forerunner of square dancing! Those identified are: 1. Fred Paul, 2. Raymond Hubbs, 3. Alfred Wolf, 4. Elsie Herring, and 5. Almira Pulling. Hoyt's was later bought by the Ferme family.

Parker Pharmacy, Central Islip, L. I.

Parker Pharmacy was quite prominent in 1908. Situated south of the railroad, it was owned by Harrison Jones and operated by John Day. A great fire broke out here in the early hours of a spring night in 1918 and demolished the entire block. The bucket brigade drew water from two cisterns. Benstock's Grocery Store, Bernstein's Dry Goods, Dickson's Butcher Shop, and Daly's Funeral Establishment were leveled.

Morris Benstock came from the border of Russia-Poland in 1905. He established a large grocery-hardware store on the corner just south of the railroad. When it was demolished in the fire of 1918, Benstock rebuilt. His son Sidney later took over the business. Harrison Jones, whose pharmacy was next door, became a hospital druggist. The Wilbur Pearsall family lived over the funeral home. All were safely rescued when the fire struck.

Two
Talk of the Town

The view is of Carlton Avenue from the railroad station c. 1940. This block was rebuilt after the great fire of 1918. Listed from left to right are as follows: Hellers Luncheonette, which first housed the Village newspaper *Talk of The Town*; Botfields (Rexall) Drug Store; Benstock's Hardware and Grocery Store; and Hirschleins (Whelan) Drug Store.

Motor Parkway is viewed from Wheeler Road in 1916. Dusty lanes and unpaved roads were not conducive to the horseless carriages that chugged through town shortly after the turn of the century. This historic road was financed partially by William K. Vanderbilt for his cup races. It extended 45 miles from New York City to Lake Ronkonkoma and was the nation's first toll road. Rich in bold new ideas, it was the forerunner of every parkway and turnpike that weaves across this nation today. Curious architects and engineers came from all over to ride on this great ribbon of concrete that pioneered road construction. It cut through the north of Central Islip.

The Motor Parkway tollgate has become Bon Wit Inn located at the intersection of Deer Park Avenue. This historic thoroughfare lost its race to progress when other paved roads wove their way eastward. The original toll of $2 dropped to 40¢. The historic road was turned over to the state in 1937. The only portion still in use is between Huntington and Lake Ronkonkoma.

Bob Wohlfarth's Dodge garage on the corner of Wheeler Road and Motor Parkway. It initiated the idea of gas availability along the parkways for it served the historic toll road as well as the village.

The Central Islip National Bank was opened on the corner of Carlton and Third Avenues in 1923. In 1958 it was bought by Franklyn National Bank. In August 1962 a larger, more spacious building was constructed in the vacant lot that had been Memorial Park. In 1974 Franklyn National became European American Bank.

The snows of yesteryear engulf an early gas station. It was located on the corner of McGrath Street and Wheeler Road. In 1925 a canopy over the gas pumps was a new innovation.

Hocker's Coal Pocket long stood on west Suffolk Avenue. Erected in 1920 by Joseph Hocker, the four-legged structure was periodically filled with coal from the coal cars. Hocker's coal, feed, and flour business, established in 1911, expanded into the largest of its kind on Long Island. His tiny office later became a relic that served Hendrickson Fuel for many years. Hocker sold out to the Grange League Federation in 1936.

Johnson's garage was Hubbs general store and kept pace with the times. In the early 1920s gas was installed. The large double canopy became a landmark on the southwest corner of Wheeler Road and Suffolk Avenue. Max Johnson and Kenneth Rhodes operated it as a DeSoto-Plymouth Agency; the Scott brothers, Roy and Edwin, eventually took it over and it became American Motors.

This is the original home of Thomas Stokes. Situated on the northeast corner of Suffolk Avenue and Church Street, it was built in 1853. In 1888 Stokes's son William enlarged the house and operated a variety store in it. In 1891 he rebuilt the house and it became the George Bothwell residence. George and his twin, John, were from Co. Fermanagh, Ireland. John owned the first cobbler shop in the hamlet.

This residence was constructed of lumber from Camp Upton. Located on west Suffolk Avenue, it served as a home for several families, including the Bonsor and Flannery families. When the camp closed wood was sold inexpensively, so John Shea constructed three such houses in the area. This structure was razed to make way for Branch Lumber to expand.

Frank's Landmark was the first commercial establishment McGowan built in the village. Initially Minna Frank leased Fisher's Hotel. She wanted to establish a business herself. The ABC Liquor Board would not issue a license unless she had the establishment in operation within six weeks. She consulted the master builder, Harold McGowan, who outlined the plan, set to work, and had her in business before the deadline. William Frank now operates a successful business here.

The camera's vantage point was looking north on Wheeler Road in 1941. The Methodist parsonage is on the left and the homes of Thomas Plant and John Power are on the right.

The Koch Building was located at the hospital entrance, on the northeast corner of Carlton Avenue and Smith Street. It was originally built as a residence that also housed Harry Koch's Insurance Agency. In 1923 his father, Albert Koch, bought 20 acres of land between St. John's Avenue and Smith Street from Auburn Realty. In 1910 Cordello Herrick, Protestant chaplain at Auburn State Prison, was intrigued with the undeveloped land in this area and made its availability known to his friends. Those who responded are known by names of streets today: Rev. Cordello Herrick, Irving Colewell, Clara Clift, Elmore Ross, John Ross, Anne Booth, and George Earle (surveyor of the original map). Note the Ford in the background.

Sam Essman was the village tailor and dry cleaner. His establishment stood on the northeast corner of Carlton Avenue and Clayton Street. The site is now part of Carpluk's Texaco Service, which was the oldest gas station in the hamlet.

Looking north on Carlton Avenue in 1940, one would see a building of many lives that housed Carlton's 5&10 for 12 years. This was its fourth life! Sal Haber and Louis Botfield were proprietors who operated it successfully. Dr. Harry Dubron, D.D.S., had an office beside it and Finn's house was beyond that. Traveling north, Panzeri's Meat Market, Greenberg's Stationery, and Sam Clark Department Store are all along the visible route. The I. Clark Agency is on the right.

A veteran's park was established on the southeast corner of Suffolk Avenue and Wheeler Road. Dedicated to the servicemen who served in World War I, it was inscribed with the names of those who served. Two men of the village lost their lives in this war, John M. Harold and James F. Tierney. The Crozier Building and firehouse are in the background of this c. 1920 image.

The Men's Club joins the Memorial Day parade. It wends its way north toward the cemeteries. The Busy Bee was long a familiar candy store patronized by the youngsters of Wheeler Road School. Situated between the school and the Methodist church, it was opened by Jacob and Bertha Markham after the Depression. In 1966 it was sold to make way for the Coventry Housing Project.

The Memorial Day parade is winding its way north on Wheeler Road. From the firehouse toward the Methodist cemetery it continues on to the St. John of God Cemetery where, at both stops, ceremonies were completed with taps and bugle! All village schoolchildren participated in the annual march.

The ladies auxiliary march north toward the cemeteries. Memorial Day ceremonies are held honoring those who gave their lives for our country. Note the roof of Hatch Home in the right background. This is one of the historic houses, built before the turn of the century.

A firetruck is shown here returning from the parade. The school on Wheeler Road was always the site of merriment after parades because the first ice cream of the season made its appearance.

In 1933 the high school was completed at the Wheeler Road site and served in that capacity for many years.

Long Island Motors was established by August Heine. Situated on the hilltop of western Suffolk Avenue in the late 1920s, it was a repair shop. The building is still in use.

Sidney Siben's home and law office was built on Wheeler Road. He practiced here between 1934 and 1943 when Uncle Sam called him into service. It was later sold to Minna Frank then to Dr. John Corcoran, D.D.S. The building is preserved on Dow Street, where it was moved to make way for the shopping center.

St. John of God School was dedicated on September 24, 1924. It opened with an enrollment of 105 youngsters taught by five Sisters of Mercy. Such personalities as Sr. M. Irene and Sr. M. Antoinette are remembered in the village for having spent many years on this mission.

St. John of God Convent was opened on Third Avenue in 1924. It was purchased by Rev. James Kennedy from Harrison Jones, druggist, and served as a convent for the Sisters of Mercy, who staffed the parish school from 1924 until 1955. Originally built by the Goshier family, it was razed in 1956 to expand the complex.

Bicycles were once as numerous as cars are today. A popular mode of transportation early in the 20th century, bikes were a necessity for those settlers in outlying areas. Mary Mernin Pulling displays her bike of the 1920s. Mary settled on Oakland Avenue with her husband, Josiah. Distance necessitated this mode of conveyance.

The Central Islip Lumber yard was located on Wheeler Road in the mid-1900s. Looking east from the railroad station in the left foreground, one can see the oblong Crozier Building facing Suffolk Avenue and the Sherwin Paint Store facing Wheeler Road. Hellers garage and the old express house are on either side of the tracks. The monument had already been moved. The roof of the general store is in the left foreground.

Looking north, one would see Sherwin Paint Store and Frank's Landmark on the right. Our gate poles attracted Hollywood who sent a delegation to photograph these telephone poles painted with stripes. This was put into silent movies in 1905. At the approach of an oncoming train the poles were pulled down manually! The operator waited in a little gatehouse between train runs. Today the gates are automated; traffic, however, still waits.

The station complex is shown here facing west in the mid-20th century. The Grange League Federation (GLF) grain elevator towers 85 feet in the left background. Built in 1938 the village skyscraper stored and processed feed and grain. It was razed in 1983. The express house serviced freight. The shelter for the gatekeeper, in the right foreground, was occupied between train runs. Wilbur Pearsall and later John Zimmerman held this position. Johnson's garage is across the road. This was the hub of activity for many years.

Opposite: The interior of the railroad station contained an office where telegrams were dispatched and received. The station master worked here between train runs, sold tickets, and announced the arrival of trains. Note the telephones of a bygone era. Founding father George K. Hubbs was first station master at this site. In a later generation, from 1923 to 1953, George Ayling was caretaker of the station.

Intermediate students at St. John of God School in 1942. Listed from left to right are as follows: (front row) Catherine Bothwell, Norah Hynes, Anne F. Pulling, Pauline Cunnias, and Nancy Piazza; (middle row) James Moloney, Michael Brennan, Barry Wynne, Peggy Lysight, Geraldine Johnson, Sophie Douz, Mary Murphy, Peggy M. McCarthy, Jack Shanley, James Madison, and Michael Florio; (top row) Charles Curto, Martin Blake, William McCrone, Simon Flannery, Kenneth Burns, Frank Spera, Arthur Southard, Michael Vecci, Michael O'Mara, and John Blomberg.

Silverpines and the Shamrock Inn were located on the same site on west Suffolk Avenue at different times. The Shamrock Inn, the first Irish pub in Suffolk County, began when Joseph Boyle of County Donegal went into business at the close of prohibition in 1933. The predominately Irish village found it a welcome meeting place where news from across the sea was shared. In 1938 the then-owner, Samuel Cox, refused to renew the lease and it became Silverpines Apartments.

Many Faces of Ireland have graced our history. Among them are Michael and Susan Brennan, the Bothwell twins (George and James), William and Mary Bryson, Nellie Cassidy, Maurice Coughlin, Patrick Deenihan, Catherine Duffy, John and Eileen Finnin, Frank Fitzgerald, Julia Gorman, Joan Griffin, Jerry Harnetta, Brian and Bridget Hynes, John and Elizabeth Johnston, Mae Kelly, William and Margaret Leach, Joseph and Annie Lowe, Gerald and Bridget Lysight, Marie McAdam, Dennis McSweeney, William and Mary Meech, William Mernin, John Moloney, Gerard and Bridget Murphy, John O'Brien, John and Helen Power, Delia Pulling, Mary Pulling, Thomas and Elizabeth Purtell, Gretta Shork, Patrick and Eileen Spillane, William and Alice Wynne, and Jerry Warde.

During the first three decades of the 20th century our little hamlet teemed with Irish immigrants. Enthusiastic, young natives of Erin responded until nearly all of Ireland's 32 counties accepted the invitation of "Come to Central Islip, good work, good pay." They brought their Celtic cultures and traditions, which blended into the American and state hospital scene. Immigration declined following the Depression.

Three

A New Frontier

The staff house of 1889 stood near Smith Street at the entrance to the hospital grounds. It was the administration offices in the experimental days of the farm colony before Central Islip became an independent entity in 1906. In a picturesque setting, amid stately pines, it had long been a familiar landmark to thousands who walked, cycled, and drove past it daily between home and work.

In 1889 140 men cleared the first 20 acres of land. They had come from Ward's Island and liked country living. Sleeping on wheat straw mattresses, rising at 5 a.m., and working a 12-hour day did not daunt these enthusiastic residents. They, with 15 employees who earned $25 a month, were here to stay.

In its early days the grounds of Central Islip State Hospital were a masterpiece. Women patients took pride in flower gardens, roads were laid out by men, and the landscaping was done under the watchful direction of George Dow. In 1887 1,000 acres of land had been purchased 1 mile south of the railroad. John McHugh's ox teams cleared the newly acquired wilderness for the first group of wooden structures, known as A, B, and C.

The original A, B, and C wooden structures were the first buildings at the hospital. Clustered around the northeast end of the grounds they housed patients for five decades. In 1940 they were replaced by brick structures that we now know as New York Tech's sunburst. This building was A-3.

Dr. George A. Smith replaced Dr. George McDonald in 1895. He reorganized the farm colony. An engineering background gave him an interest in building and housing. The institution became independent and expanded from a small establishment of 1,000 to a complex housing 7,500 patients during his 37-year administration. Always cooperative with the local community he instituted vaudeville entertainment, a band, parties, dances, and talent shows.

The Administration Building was constructed after the hospital became independent in 1905. Central Islip State Hospital was a successful experiment meant to alleviate overcrowded conditions in city institutions. Outdoor work was considered therapy. Bicycles that transported attendants from town had to be left at the staff house and later at the Administration Building, as bicycle riding was not permitted on the hospital grounds.

The first tuberculosis building of 1903 was in North Colony. In 1911 the TB camp was relocated behind South Colony among the pines because pines played a major role in early treatment. Pine trees were brought into the wards and pine needles were used to stuff pillows. Imagine sleeping on a pine needle pillow?

Land was initially plowed on the west side of Carlton Avenue where a huge farm was established. Ninety-five percent of the patients were on the work force.

Planting was executed by the men. Work was not carried to the extent of hard labor but it was sufficient to hold the attention of the patient and give him a sense of accomplishment. Much of the produce grown here was shipped to city institutions.

Caring for plants, both outside and inside, was also a form of therapy. This was executed under the guidance of George Dow. The occupational department assisted patients in finding an occupation that he or she could excel at, while deriving pleasure and satisfaction from the work. Gardening was a useful occupation.

Group D, State Hospital, Central Islip, L. I.

Pub. by Parker Pharm

"D" buildings were the first brick structures at the farm colony. Constructed northeast of the original A, B, and C buildings, they were an asset by the mid-1890s, for the patient population had reached 1,000.

The old amusement hall was established in 1905. The forerunner of Robbins Hall, it provided entertainment until it was destroyed by fire in 1930.

A concert on the green was attractive to patients and staff alike. Outdoor concerts in the summertime were quite common and enjoyable. This one is performed between the McGreggor (M) buildings and the Smith (S) group of six buildings. Both M and S were constructed in 1913.

Calisthenics was a common form of gymnastics. Outdoor activity was a vital ingredient of recovery. The most popular prescription for healing was occupation, oxygen, rest, and recreation!

The hospital band plays for the opening of field day. This band was formed under the jurisdiction of Dr. Smith and consisted of patients. When it played in the bandstand on summer evenings the music could be heard in the village. There was a marching band, dancing band, concert band, and a symphony orchestra. Opening ceremonies took place on the ball field.

A soldier returns from military service in World War I. Dr. Smith personally greeted each returning veteran. Josiah J. Pulling was one of the youngest members of the hospital staff when, in 1910, he became a pageboy. This position has been taken over by telephones! Fifteen years later he was the switchboard operator on night duty when he met his wife, Mary Mernin, of Co. Waterford.

Dr. David Corcoran was appointed third director of Central Islip State Hospital. He served from 1933 until 1946. During his tenure the old A, B, and C buildings were replaced. An Irish-American club was formed among the employees and the stadium was laid out. During the war years many male employees were called into military service which created a shortage of men. Lengthened sessions on duty became common.

Kitchen #4 of the L group supplied work to staff and patients for many years. It has retained its identity into a new era for it has become a culinary school.

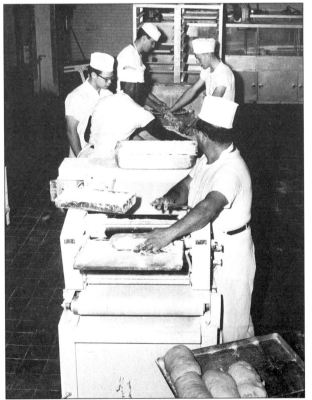

The bakery dated back before the turn of the century and provided employment from earliest times. Thomas Miller was first head baker. The bakery was later relocated to the northern end of the storehouse.

In 1940 the new A, B, and C buildings replaced the original wooden structures. These buildings were originally used as residences, as the institution had reached a population of 7,826 patients. In a new era the structures, which form a semicircle, serve as the administrative offices and library of the New York Institute of Technology. They are now known as Sunburst.

Hoffman House was built as a residence for doctors in 1911. It was named after a hotel in New York during the gay 1890s. The Viele Home and North Colony Home were built for the staff.

Civil Defense drills were held on the hospital grounds. Our underground tunnels were designated bomb shelters for the hospital patients and personnel as well as for neighboring towns.

The Administration Building was the ideal place to erect an observation tower during World War II. Central Islip's proximity to the sea made the area subject to attack. This is a back view of the building.

This observation tower, built for plane spotting and manned by employee volunteers, was located on the Administration Building during World War II. The planes that flew over Long Island during that era were those being tested by Grumman and Republic Aircraft Factories before being sent overseas.

The Honor Roll of employees who answered the call of Uncle Sam during World War II. The decreased employee population necessitated remaining men to work 12-hour shifts. All employees were expected to report for duty in the event of an air raid.

The class of 1908 was the second class to graduate from Central Islip. The school of nursing, begun in 1896, was expanded in 1921 to incorporate a three-year program. There was a three-month course for attendants. Prior to 1906 graduations were held at Manhattan State Hospital, Ward's Island.

Pictured are the 1926 graduates of the school of nursing. Carter Woods, William P. Mernin, Anne Laughlin, Mrs. Givney (who later became president of the school of nursing), Rose Devine, Thomas Boyd, Susan Cassidy Brennan, and Julia Marshall.

The carpenter shop turned out furniture as well as smaller items to sell at the annual hospital fairs. Much of the furniture throughout the buildings was made here. Straight back chairs, made in these shops, were common throughout state institutions.

The print shop turned out all the forms, notices, and letterhead used throughout the hospital. Patients also printed the hospital newspaper.

The hospital engine and crew were captured in this 1934 image—Frank Rhodes was a trainman; Frank Alling, conductor; Jacob Acker, engineer; Mike Callahan, fireman; and Walter Webb, conductor. The train, purchased from the railroad in 1909, shuttled among the hospital buildings transporting food, laundry, and supplies. It made daily trips to the railroad station in Central Islip for express parcels.

The first steam engine chugged into the hospital grounds in 1909. It consisted of an engine, a baggage car, and later a passenger coach was added. On "transfer days" the coach went to the city on the train from Central Islip and returned in the evening with new patients. The train was discontinued in 1934 when bus travel was initiated.

The station at the hospital also served as an express house. Situated along the north side of the grounds, it was a point of distribution to various parts of the institution. The boiler house smokestack can be seen in the distance.

The Smith Group was completed in 1911. Consisting of six, two-story cottages, it accommodated 600 residents. By this time the patient population had reached 4,154.

This is the South Colony's "H" dining room in 1938, one of many such dining rooms spread over the mile-long establishment. They were attractively decorated in keeping with the season.

Robbins Hall replaced the old amusement hall in 1930. The building was named for Harry Robbins, a member of the board of managers. Physical training classes, parties, dances, roller skating jamborees, costume balls, and special events were all part of the therapeutic process.

The interior of Robbins Hall has a seating capacity of 1,700 and was completed in 1931. Movie projectors were installed in 1933 and the village youngsters looked forward to Saturday morning performances. The first movie was attended by 700 patients. Social events were frequent and considered recreational therapy.

It's showtime in Robbins Hall! This was one of many performances presented on the Robbins Hall stage. During the early and mid-1900s this was considered a beneficial practice. This production occurred on November 25, 1941.

Numerous entertainments took place in Robbins Hall. Complete with a band, this performance celebrates Washington's birthday. The entire cast and band were recovering patients.

Patients dance the Virginia Reel. Through recreational therapy, social training, and physical training, 95 percent of all patients were reached and rehabilitated. This is a specifically prescribed therapy.

The bowling alley was in Robbins Hall. It provided an aspect of rehabilitation that was therapeutic as well as pleasurable. Patients await a turn to try their luck.

The superintendent's residence was built in a picturesque setting. Situated on a hill along the west side of Carlton Avenue, the landscaping surrounding it was the result of occupational therapy. The site now encompasses the Bishop McGann housing project.

Dr. Francis J. O'Neill was a native of Vermont. He graduated from the University of Vermont Medical School and the Columbia School of Physicians and Surgeons. He served as director at Central Islip from 1946 until 1972 and steered the Psychiatric Center through its most turbulent era. Dr. O'Neill initially served with the Naval Hospital Mobile Unit in the South Pacific. He was medical officer on the battleship *Missouri* on August 14, 1945, and witnessed the signing of the historic treaty "Japan Surrenders."

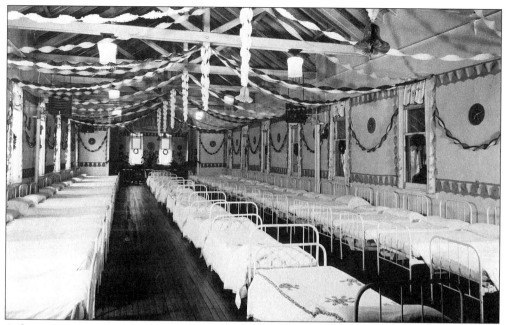

A dorm scene in 1940 indicates an overcrowded but neat ward. Patients slept in dormitories, or wards. An attendant assumed night duty, which lasted from midnight until eight the next morning. This time span was extended during the war years on the male wards.

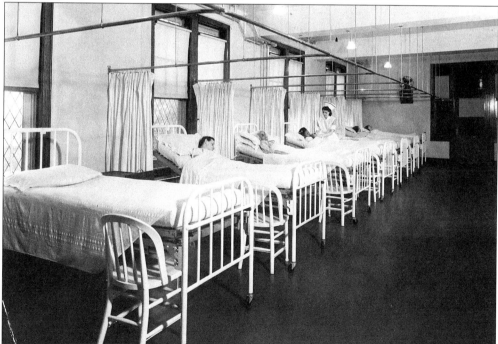

In 1922 a housing project for an additional thousand patients was opened. Known as the James Group, in 1929 the "J" building of that project was designated as the infirmary. This relieved small clinical units throughout the hospital. Residents requiring hospital care were housed on the first and second floors. The third floor was specifically for employees.

An employee relaxes in his room in the Viele Home. Constructed in 1911 along Carlton Avenue beside the amusement hall, it was named for a member of the board of directors and provided housing for 216 new employees in the early days of the hospital. A section of the B unit also provided living quarters for new employees.

A group of employees visit Marcy State Hospital in upstate NY. Listed from left to right are as follows: (front row) Betty Scott, Mary Ryan, Jean Melton, and Adeline Cassidy; (back row) Steve Tesoro, Ann Tesoro, John Crotty, and Rose Holmes.

Hospital employees gather for a break. Here Marie McAdam, Mae Kelly, Eileen Spillane, and Julia Gorman have a chat. Patient population increased during the first six decades of the 20th century, reaching a peak of ten thousand in 1955.

Bridget Murphy is shown here wearing her attendant uniform of gray and white. This was a familiar scene around town. Village life centered around the hospital because it provided employment. Many Irish immigrants answered the call to Central Islip. Bridget is a native of Limerick City.

Jack Johnston receives a word of congratulations from Dr. Francis O'Neill, director. Jack has completed a half-century of service to the state. A 1914 graduate of the school of nursing, he was a supervisor and charge nurse. Jack originally had a ticket for the *Titanic* and fortunately he was denied passage. The next liner brought him safely through the Golden Gates. He served in the infantry during World War I.

Leo Frey admires his little granddaughter, Jackie Frey. A native of upstate New York, Frey was appointed chief steward of Central Islip State Hospital in 1931. He held this position until his death in 1961. He was revered by employees, staff, and residents alike.

The stadium at Central Islip comes alive at game time. In 1933 a baseball diamond and stadium were constructed and enjoyed by both patients and employees alike. Visiting teams were always welcome. Michael VanDitto had the stadium laid out by John Stepsis, the golf course by Thomas O'Neill, and the ball field by Peter Milhaven. All are currently in operation.

Dr. David Corcoran, third director of the hospital, throws out the first ball. Teams from other towns used our ball field for competition games and sometimes played our team.

Warm up time for twirlers and the band before going out on parade. Scenes such as this were common preceding field day or anytime the band was called upon to play. Residents considered practice just as solemn as the real performance. This parade is complete with a lighthouse float. Performances usually resulted in awards, trophies, and happy residents with a sense of accomplishment.

A Memorial Day parade marches north on Wheeler Road toward the cemeteries where ceremonies will be conducted. The house in the background is that of Samuel Hatch, caretaker on the Slater estate. In later years his daughter, Ruth, owned it. The house is among those preserved on Dow Street.

Central Islip was always proud of its baseball team. The first hospital team was the Braves of 1933. Listed from left to right the team is as follows: (front row) Howard Lindquist, ? Walker, Richard Fritchie, Frank Keating, Eddie McGrath, and Frank Fitzpatrick; (back row) Gene Schultz, Douglas Dixon, Fred Herring, Frank McCourt, Almon Scott, and Jim Mattern.

Gull Haven Country Clubhouse has ben popular for years. Thomas Elsbee, Frank Sicilian, and John Berniaz, all of neighboring hamlets, warm up before heading out for a round on the course. The Town of Islip currently owns the clubhouse and golf course. Both were once part of the local hospital. Seagulls, from nearby Great South Bay, seem to know they belong here, hence the name.

Arthur Weingattner is ready to tee it up on the first hole. The old guardhouse is in the background.

The guardhouse of a bygone era. This tiny five-sided structure, which long stood at the entrance to the hospital grounds near Smith Street, is preserved at the Gull Haven Country Club. A nostalgic remnant of village history, many employees traveled past it twice daily and many others sought refuge within its walls to enjoy a few moments with a friend. The establishment it guarded for nearly a century has now vanished into antiquity.

Four
Village Expansion

This mini mall, located along east Suffolk Avenue, was built by Harold McGowan in 1946. Known as B & B, or Benstock and Bernstein, it housed the first supermarket in the hamlet and initiated shopping carts into the village. In order to complete this series of buildings in the allotted time, one continuous foundation was erected from the colonial post office at the west end to the variety store at the east end.

McGowan's mini mall of 1946 began with a colonial post office. Situated along northeast Suffolk Avenue, the row of stores extended to Church Street. Towering pines once sheltered Holmes's and later Dr. Earl McCoy's residence on this corner. The post office moved from Carlton Avenue in 1947.

In 1953 McGowan extended his mini mall west to the corner of Wheeler Road. Page Drugs opened in 1954, and has since occupied that corner. The colonial post office is five buildings east in front of the tree.

The offices of Harold McGowan were housed in the old Guild Hall on East Suffolk Avenue across from his mini mall. Later the building became a sweet shop and still later a Carvel store. The row of stores extended west to the original firehouse facing the mini mall.

This shopping center was located along the south side of east Suffolk Avenue. It extended from the McGowan offices to the original firehouse. Industry had come to town in the form of a thrift shop, the Central Islip Furniture Store, a laundromat, and Post Radio Repair. These were just a few of the newcomers of that era.

Harold McGowan envisioned expansion for the hamlet in 1932. A master builder, he created phenomenal housing developments. Homes sprouted rapidly around town and many continue to be inhabited. His achievements are legion. He is a scientist, sculptor, musician, world traveler, author, and a master builder. This Doctor of Science is a member of MENSA, the Explorers Club, was chairman of the Board of Atomic Research, and is listed in *Who's Who In The World*.

The McGowan Shopping Center on northeast Suffolk Avenue is shown here in 1948. Suffolk Variety Store long occupied the corner of Suffolk Avenue and Church Street. This was the original site of the Episcopal church.

This 1960 aerial view facing west shows the new Woolworths shopping center. McGowan's mini mall faces the original firehouse (white building). The GLF towers are in the upper left of this image. The general store faces east at the intersection of Suffolk Avenue and Wheeler Road. In the right foreground the Dollar Store and parking lot on east Suffolk Avenue are visible.

The monument to World War I veterans stands on a new site. Complete with a cannon it was relocated, in the 1950s, to a park beside the Central Islip National Bank on the corner of Carlton and Third Avenues.

A monument was obtained honoring the servicemen of World War II. Together the monuments stood in the Carlton Avenue Park for over a decade. They were later moved to the school grounds on Wheeler Road to make way for the bank to expand.

The high school band marches north on Wheeler Road. Schoolchildren follow the line of march. This was an annual ritual in Central Islip on Memorial Day.

The veterans of foreign wars march north toward the cemeteries. Here, each Memorial Day, ceremonies are held honoring those who lost their lives for our country. Note the roof of the Hatch Home in the right background. This is one of the historic houses preserved on Dow Street.

A last glimpse of the old railroad station before demolition. The station house is in the foreground. Looking east one detects the new mini mall beyond the Tydol sign. The steeple of the original firehouse rises above the lumberyard. This was the scene just before the original station vanished from the landscape in 1954.

A temporary railroad station was erected just west of the old one. Constructed of cinder blocks it began operation in June 1959. Harold McGowan had constructed a mini mall across the road. The cinder block station was short lived.

Woolworth's shopping center is shown here on the northwest corner of Wheeler Road and Suffolk Avenue in 1955. It was built on the site of two original houses, which are preserved on Dow Street.

A motion picture theater was established on the corner of Carlton Avenue and Clayton Street in 1950. It was a chain of Associated Prudential Theaters with a seating capacity of 593. Staffed by local residents, it remained in operation for 15 years.

The Wheeler Road School was renamed for Anthony Alfano. He served on the board of education for many years. In 1950 an extensive wing was added to the original 1913 building to accommodate the rising enrollment.

Central Islip Senior High School was opened on Wheeler Road in September 1970 with an enrollment of 1,921.

Suffolk Wayside Furniture Shop has stood on Carlton Avenue since 1946. John Bartell and Frank Fitzpatrick operated a successful furniture business at this site for many years.

A new firehouse on Carlton Avenue was completed in 1937. It housed six trucks for an expanding population. Station #2 on Wheeler Road was opened in 1963 and Station #3, across Veteran's Highway, opened in 1972.

The blizzard of December 26, 1947, transformed Oakland Avenue into a winter wonderland. A view north indicates the road has not yet been cut through. William Bryson's garage is on the right.

Oakland Avenue is shown here photographed a half-century later from Suffolk Avenue. The road has been cut through to Motor Parkway and housing projects have developed along Oakland Avenue. For many years this road terminated just left of the woodland.

Watral's Homestead is located on west Suffolk Avenue. Originally it was James Geary's summer home and the site of the first Catholic mass in the village, which was celebrated July 3, 1895, by Rev. Henry F. Murray, the pastor of St. Anne's in Brentwood. St. John's was eight years in the future. Then it became Fred Moquot's summer farmhouse. John Watral bought it in 1935 and established a huge dairy farm which his son Michael operated.

Michael Watral was the village milkman. He built his business into a modern dairy empire. Watral Farms was long famous for its "Grade A Milk." In 1943 he joined the fire department and in 1950 was elected fire chief. He served six, five-year terms as fire commissioner. In 1960 his dairy business evolved into a construction enterprise. It is to his credit that all four of his sons chose to work with him.

We gathered at Walsh's yard each Christmas. This tiny church, placed by Thomas Walsh Sr. beside his funeral establishment, created a fascination during the war years. He piped Christmas music through a loud speaker from his living room, over the funeral home, and into the miniature church. It lit up while the melodies echoed through the village. It was a first of its kind!

The Walsh Funeral Home was established by Robert McBreen in 1906. Six years later the building was erected on a parcel of the Slater estate. In 1930, following McBreen's death, Thomas Walsh Sr. bought the business. He was a prominent mortician for three decades. The torch was passed on to his son, Thomas Jr., who took it over in 1963. In 1970 a new wing was added on the north side of the building.

The Moloney Funeral Home was established on Carlton Avenue in 1934. James J. Moloney Sr. was a notable, Irish mortician who operated the business successfully for 25 years. In 1960 his son Jack became proprietor and during his tenure the building was enlarged. In 1985 it was sold to Jack's brother, F. Daniel Moloney. The family now has five funeral homes, eight active funeral directors, and their own crematory.

The Queen of All Saints Diocesan Cemetery was dedicated on November 1, 1982, by Bishop John R. McGann. Located beside the St. John of God Cemetery it serves the catholic population in the Diocese of Rockville Centre.

Anne Pfifferling was the first republican woman to hold public office in the Town of Islip. In 1969 she began a seven-year tenure as town clerk and in 1976 was elected councilwoman becoming the first woman, in any party, to receive this distinction. Anne inherited much of her political interest from her father, Vern Furman, who was active in civic affairs. He served as justice of the peace and supervisor of the Town of Islip.

Mary J. Finnin is a graduate of Central Islip School of Nursing, class of 1956. She received the Harry P. Robbins award. In 1978 Mary was summoned back to Robbins Hall to deliver the final address as the school of nursing phased into history. Mary went on to attain a B.S.N. from Adlephi and a M.S.N. from St. John's University. She was elected to The American Nurses Association of Directors in 1980.

John Finnerty was in the Coast Guard Intelligence Service. He intercepted spies at Amagansette during World War II. He was a professor of criminology and director of Suffolk County Probation Department. Finnerty was an instructor in Farmingdale Police Academy and served as resource consultant for the White House Conference on Crime. In 1971 he was elected councilman for the Town of Islip and in 1976 was elected sheriff, a position he held for two terms.

Nicholas Ezzo's house is on the right and Biehl's home is on the left of Brightside Avenue. There was once a huge lumber yard here. Maple trees were planted on Brightside Avenue by George W. Bridger, who was interested in the civic development of the community before the turn of the century. The trees formed a natural arch over the street. Many of these trees have survived.

Expansion reached the St. John of God Parish in 1954. A new wing was added to the school. The golden jubilee of the parish and the dedication of the new wing coincided. The interior of the church was renovated and the hall was first used for Sunday services. In this 1955 aerial view, the Mercy Convent is in the left background. The church was built in 1903 and the rectory in 1906.

During the days of expansion the Mercy Convent on Third Avenue was razed and a new one built on St. John's Avenue. In 1955 a transfer of religious communities took place. Due to the proximity of St. Joseph's College in Brentwood, the Sisters of St. Joseph came to staff the school and the Sisters of Mercy opened St. Martin's in Bethpage.

The McAllister property is pictured here in 1974. In November of that year work was begun on the new library. Located on the east side of Hawthorne Avenue, the chosen site had been the wooded property of Richard McAllister. After being researched for several years the location was deemed accessible to the schools. A picturesque setting remained with a new dimension.

The library was rising rapidly. The dimensions are established and the fireproof masonry ready for placement. This is six months into the project on April 1975.

This is the Central Islip Public Library. Sometimes referred to as the bicentennial library, it was opened on March 15, 1976, with a capacity of 100,000 volumes on 20,000 square feet of space. Circulation reached over 7,000 with 950 patrons in the first two weeks. The library was dedicated on May 2, 1976.

Joseph Vecci seals the cornerstone of the new library on May 2, 1976, following the dedication ceremony. The cornerstone contains current newspapers, periodicals, memorabilia, and a copy of the new village history, which was published for the bicentennial. Elizabeth Gordon was librarian and Marion Kowalczyk assistant.

Librarian Elizabeth Gordon poses with Councilman Norman DeMott, Claudia Daileader, Kenneth Rhodes, Dorothy Wagner, Mrs. Harry Herman, and Henry Hocker at the entrance to the new state-of-the-art library.

Josiah J. Pulling, father of the author; Marian Kowalczyk, assistant librarian; Larry LoValley, publisher; Elizabeth Gordon, librarian; and Sr. Anne Frances Pulling, author, review the newly published history of Central Islip which made its debut with the new library.

Claude Horrell, mayor of Islip, England, came on a goodwill visit during our bicentennial. His home, the ancestral home of William Nicholl, is located 70 miles north of London on the River Avon. In 1683 Nicholl bought land from the Connequot Indians and named his Long Island estate Islip. Chatting with Josiah J. Pulling, Horrell said he hoped to see the places pictured in *Central Islip, My Hometown* to make the book come alive.

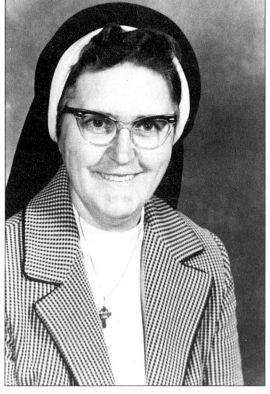

Sr. Anne Frances Pulling R.S.M., M.A. is a member of the Sisters of Mercy. A graduate of College Misericordia in Dallas, PA, and Fordham University, she entered the Sisters of Mercy in 1948. Sister Anne Frances has pursued a lifelong teaching career throughout New York and Pennsylvania. She has authored several books including *Central Islip My Hometown* in 1976.

Five

Recycling, Renewal, Rebirth

The Bishop McGann Village is a Catholic Charities Senior Citizen Housing Complex of the Roman Catholic Diocese of Rockville Center. One hundred and twenty-five affordable rental units were constructed on 8 acres of land along the west side of Carlton Avenue. The Bishop was honored for his years of work providing affordable housing for seniors.

Joan Johnson was the first African-American elected to office in Islip in over 300 years. She has been reelected three times. Joan is the recipient of many public and community service awards including the Role Model Award from The National Council of Negro Women and the Clara Barton Award from the Red Cross.

Michael LoGrande, planning director and Islip town supervisor, was instrumental in bringing in a university that would anchor and stabilize research and development.

Charles and Jeanette Reed pose with their son, Rev. Bruce Reed. He is assistant pastor of St. Vincent de Paul Roman Catholic Church in Elmont, Long Island. Father Bruce is the first African-American ordained to the priesthood for the Diocese of Rockville Centre. As a seminarian he walked 3,000 miles on a peace march through 12 states. His biracial background is an asset to his ministry. He was ordained on May 29, 1992.

The McCalla family is pictured here. Kim, an engineer, was assistant project manager of the stadium at Baltimore Convention Center. Christopher is a pilot for United Airlines and is one of the few African-Americans to fly a F15 fighter plane. Ruth is a veterinarian and Richard is a General Contractor for the Town of Islip revitalization project.

The Hope Missionary Baptist Church was established in 1959. Situated on Lemon Street it serves the growing black population. Rev. Richard Loving was founding pastor.

This is the new Methodist church on Wheeler Road. By 1966 the congregation had outgrown the wooden church of 1870. The increasing membership necessitated a new modern church. This was constructed across Wheeler Road. The historic structure is under consideration for refurbishment.

This is the ground-breaking ceremony for the federal courthouse. Situated at the southern end of the college campus, the 25-acre site next to the Cohalan Complex provides permanent employment for the area. The 450,000-square-foot complex was begun in 1995.

Marisabel Morales of Central Islip leads the Star Spangled Banner at the official dedication of the federal courts. Judge Wexler, Congressman Lazio, and County Executive Gaffney with other officials look on.

Randy Cardona accepts a $1,100 scholarship check from Barbara Walsh, civic council treasurer. Also pictured are Randy's mother, President Hank Carney, and Judy and Philip Benson. Randy now attends Fordham University where he has a football scholarship. He was chosen for his academic achievement. Administered by the civic council, the Brian Benson Scholarship was created by the Bensons in memory of their son, Brian.

Governor Cuomo congratulates members of the Clean Team who helped refurbish the village through awareness and landscaping. The project affords summer employment to high school students.

Louis Majore celebrates his 89th birthday with Hank Carney, president of the civic council; Nancy Manfredonia, executive director of the civic association; Jack Agai, past president; Lillian Modica; Norman DeMott, councilman; and Gerline Ridges. Lou, Lillian, and Gerline are residents of the Senior Congregate Complex on Lowell Avenue managed by the civic council. Lou is a former NYC taxi driver.

Joan Oscar, Rev. Bruce Reed, and Lora Philips were the village representation at the National Black Catholic Congress held at the convention center in Baltimore.

Llamas visit the Summer Reading Program at the Central Islip Public Library. Children are encouraged to use the library during the summer months to keep reading skills sharp! Many children in the village take advantage of this resource.

Story time for the youngsters at Central Islip Public Library. There are many activities offered here throughout the year, including drama and parent-toddler workshops, story time at various levels, and class visits from local schools.

This is a college woods street scene following revitalization. In its new career, the once blighted area enjoys a landscaped environment. Previously known as Carlton Park, the area has been recycled from a ghetto to a vibrant and attractive neighborhood of affordable and attractive homes.

The Central Islip Civic Council banner is proudly displayed following the Memorial Day parade. Ruth Johnson, town clerk, and Congressman Richard Lazio join with friends. This diverse ethnic gathering is characteristic of the hamlet.

The Fire Belles of Central Islip proudly carry their banner north on Wheeler Road as they perform in the Memorial Day parade.

The historic Charles Heines homestead on Wheeler Road was built in 1888. Renovations are restoring the building to its original clapboard, Victorian style. Included in the purchase, by the Central Islip Civic Council, is the blacksmith shop of Henry Heines, a barn, and several acres of land. The Town of Islip has designated the complex a Landmark Preservation District.

Six

A Renaissance
Village Emerges

The railroad station moved east again. In 1988 an electrified railway to Manhattan was installed along the main line. The railroad station, originally located at the Islip Avenue crossing in 1842, was moved east to the Carlton Avenue crossing in 1874 where it remained for over a century. Traffic congestion deemed it advisable to move east again to Lowell Avenue. The train reaches New York City in less than an hour.

The post office has been housed in various locations. First there were ten mailboxes in the general store. In 1923 the post office moved to Carlton Avenue and remained there until 1946, when Harold McGowan designed a colonial post office on east Suffolk Avenue. Seventeen years in these quarters and the post office moved east to a larger building that served until the 1990s, when this huge building was erected to serve Islandia as well as Central Islip.

A new firehouse was constructed on the west side of Carlton Avenue in 1992. It contains many new features such as space for a larger pump and rescue vehicles, extra bays, a double bay for truck maintenance, a fire school lecture room, conference rooms, a fully equipped kitchen, trophy area, and the necessities that would assure the continuous presence of a dispatcher.

David and Ellen Ehrlich Scarbrick are graduates of the Central Islip schools Class of 1975. David is a neurological psychologist. Ellen is an internationally certified radiological technologist. They live and practice in the Poconos. They have two children, David and Diana.

Dr. Andrew G. Schwartz, D.D.S., bought the practice of Dr. Jacklyn on Wheeler Road in 1986. Schwartz is a graduate of Columbia University School of Dentistry. He served as president of the chamber of commerce from 1989 to 1992, and was vice president of the Lions Club. He appreciates the master plan that includes housing, education, business, and retail development in Central Islip. He teaches at the State University in Stony Brook.

111

Principal and Colonel Jack Cassidy address youngsters at the Ralph Reed Junior High School on career day. A Vietnam veteran, Cassidy participated in active fighting and received many awards among which were the silver star, the bronze star, and the purple heart. He spent 32 years, active and reserve, in the Marine Corps. Cassidy is a graduate of Central Islip High School and Post College/University. He has been the principal of Reed School for the past two decades.

John DiClemente, assistant principal, and John Smith, principal of the senior high school, were once students in the local schools. Among others are as follows: Carin Baxter Velaquez, Tom Helmke, Everett Melvis, John Shaughnesy, Jim Mott, Greg Alpers, Mike Stein, Stephen Zagorsky, Tony Antonucci, Jerry Watkins, Chris Pisano, and Tony Pavek. It is to the credit of the Central Islip public schools that so many of its graduates seek employment in Central Islip.

Monica Cintron and Kevin Chesnov receive honors at the seventh-grade award assembly at the Ralph Reed School. Principal Jack Cassidy has a word of congratulations for them. Awards are conferred throughout the year to deserving students. Doctor Ralph Reed, for whom the school was named, was originally on the staff of the state hospital. He went into private practice in 1927, served the village for many years, and was the school physician.

Roller hockey was introduced into the St. John of God Parish in the middle of the 20th century. It has been an attraction for young lads of the village and has provided sportsmanship for several generations of youngsters. The handsome young gentleman behind the mask is Albert Hanes.

Memorial Park has moved around the village in its eight-decade history. It has currently found a niche in front of the administrative offices, which comprise the schoolhouse of 1913, the high school of 1933, and the elementary school of a later vintage. A space capsule was buried at this site in 1983 commemorating 300 years of the town of Islip. The capsule contains memorabilia of the era.

The Admissions Building of former times awaits its destiny. Thousands of residents have been admitted through this structure at the south end of the campus. Through an unique twist of destiny the Central Islip State Hospital, which provided employment for nearly a century, has become a career-oriented, hands-on college with access to opportunity and service in public interest.

This is a nostalgic flashback during a transitional era. Groups A and B once housed residents of the state hospital. In the new lifetime of A and B they house the administration offices and the Library of the New York Institute of Technology, known as Sunburst.

This was an infirmary serving the medical needs of both staff and residents from 1929 through 1972. It now houses offices, classrooms, computer labs, and the maintenance department of the college. The buildings lend themselves to the mission of the school. Students have opportunities to gain work experience through course work. The New York Institute of Technology was founded in Westbury in 1955. The Central Islip campus opened in 1984 with 350 students.

The "L" dining room of old has entered a new era. In a modern generation it has been transformed into a Culinary Arts School, dining hall, and restaurant. Here, students have an opportunity to advance culinary skills with hands on experience while studying!

Chefs of the future learn the techniques of culinary art. the New York Institute of Technology provides career opportunities in hotel, restaurant, hospital, and institutional food service as well as in banquet and catering pursuits.

The library of the New York Institute of Technology is fully equipped to prepare students for the challenges of the 21st century. The capability of this tool, the computer, is rapidly increasing. Access to computers is available throughout the campus.

Sports are enjoyed on the Islip campus. the New York Institute of Technology offers intercollegiate, athletic, and varsity programs in basketball, soccer, lacrosse, volley ball, track, and baseball.

The Student Activities Center was the rehabilitative unit. It has become the recreational center of the New York Institute of Technology. It houses a full fitness room, a gym, pool, theater, canteen, and stage.

The stadium at Central Islip has acquired a new lease on life. Under the jurisdiction of the Town of Islip, it has become a source of recreational opportunity for the college community as well as for townsfolk.

Students gather for a few moments to compare notes, share stories, or just for fun and relaxation.

Park Row is viewed from the south. This is a middle-income housing development situated on what was North Colony. Progress brought advances in medical-psychiatric practices and the Farm Colony of 1889 had successfully fulfilled its mission as it phased into history.

A tree-lined island separates the New York Institute of Technology from Park Row. In earlier times this was part of North Colony. Decentralization heralded the decline of state institutions.

A sign, artistically embedded into the earth, heralds an innovative and vibrant lifetime in the annals of this site! The stadium is in the background.

Seven
Meet Our Neighbors

The sun sets over Lake Ronkonkoma. A freshwater lake formed during the glacial age evolved into a resort. The railroad and Motor Parkway gave rise to its prosperity when notable celebrities summered in Lakeland. Raynor Beach dates back to 1840. Seasonal crowds grew and beaches were established complete with boarding houses, hotels, picnic groves, and pavilions. The Hollywood Pavilion and Green Pavilion offered live entertainment. Duffields West park became Islip Town Beach.

The Cenacle Retreat House in Ronkonkoma was established in 1922, but the main building wasn't completed until November 1927. The Cenacle hosts various and diverse programs, retreats, weekend retreats, workshops, etc. This was once the Adams estate. The home of Maude Adams was the convent of the sisters during their first five years in Ronkonkoma.

This was the home of Maude Adams, the actress who made Peter Pan famous when it was produced in 1904. She was a weekend visitor to her Ronkonkoma estate since 1898. The Cenacle Sisters in New York cared for her through a serious illness. She deeded her estate to the Sisters for a Cenacle in the country and lived here until her death in 1953. The house still stands on the Cenacle property.

The Methodist church of Hauppauge was built in 1806. The names Wheeler, Hubbs, Nichols, Smith, and Miller are among the church's founders. The oak trees surrounding the church were preserved as shade for the horses during services. In 1895 the steeple and bell were added. Town Line Road, on which the church long stood, was laid out in 1789 by the commissioners of both the towns of Smithtown and Islip.

This sleigh ride from the Cornish House in Hauppauge took place about 1912. Located on Town Line Road, the Methodist church is visible on the left. Warren Hubbs is the driver with Adelia Smith Haynes beside him. Sarah J. Soper and Harriet Cornish are in back with Miss Cornish standing beside them. This picture and sleigh are on display in the Carriage Museum of Stony Brook.

Locustdale was a summer camp for children. Youngsters from the Brooklyn Home for Children summered here at the turn of the century. Locustdale was located at the point where the road divides. Later a Texaco Station, Robert Hall Clothing, and Shoe Town would occupy this prestigious point.

This charming chateau was located on Carlton Avenue in East Islip. The Irish Coffee House founded in 1983 offers the finest food and Irish entertainment. One has the choice of an exquisite Waterford crystal room, an elegant Roscommon room with a terrace, or any of its beautiful banquet rooms. In a tradition of excellence, the atmosphere befits the culture kept alive in such a setting.

the Islandia Town Hall on Old Nicholls Road serves a hamlet of 2.25 square miles with a population of 2,769 inhabitants. It lies just across Veterans Highway to our east. It was carved from Central Islip, Hauppauge, and Ronkonkoma when a vote to incorporate the village was approved in 1985. There are three school districts, fire districts, and postal districts within the village.

The Islandia Shopping Center was established in 1991. Situated in a spacious setting, it covers a vast area and affords variety to shoppers. Computer Associates World headquarters was established on Motor Parkway in Islandia. Thirteen hundred seventy-seven Motor Parkway is a copper-colored, glass office building. It dominates the landscape on the corner of Motor Parkway and Veterans Highway just across from the shopping center.

Captree Bridge spans Great South Bay. Four miles south of Central Islip the sea becomes our neighbor. The double bridge over the bay provides easy access to the Atlantic Ocean. Swimming and fishing are prevalent in the area. Situated just off Montauk Highway in West Islip, the project was undertaken by Robert Moses and features an Ocean Drive between the ocean and the bay.

Sailboats cruise Great South Bay at the East Islip Marina. Mooring is situated beside East Islip Beach. This was an attraction to youngsters of earlier times. In the days before swimming pools were popular it was a sport in the summertime to cycle from Central Islip to the beach for a swim.

Brentwood, the "Village of Modern Times," lies to our west. In 1851 social reformers established an utopian colony designed to revolutionize human society. Chosen for its pure water and pine forests, it became the site of an ambitious, social experiment that promoted positivism. Two relics of that era still grace the landscape. They are the stately towering pines that were planted by the early settlers of Modern Times and the octagonal house.

The octagonal house stood on the east side of Brentwood Road since the 1860s. William Dame, a cabinetmaker from Boston, came to join the utopian existence of Modern Times. He built this eight-sided dwelling and explained that by eliminating acute angles he had economized on space. Modern Times phased out after the Civil War. The area was renamed Brentwood.

St. Joseph's Academy was established in Pine Park. The Austral Hotel, built in 1888 as a resort, experienced an unique twist of destiny that assured Brentwood a prominent place in religious and educational history. In 1896 the Austral became the convent of the Sisters of St. Joseph. In 1903 the academy building was complete and in 1911 it was extended to accommodate rising enrollment.

A century later St. Joseph's golden complex majestically stretches among the pines. The convent building of 1929 and Sacred Heart Chapel of 1930, with its beautiful campanile and carillon chimes, completed the original complex. In 1955 Brentwood College was added and now houses a branch of Post College. St. Joseph's has always offered quality education to students at home as well as many countries abroad. Brentwood has become synonymous with educational excellence on all levels.